Writing about Music

A Style Sheet
from the editors of
19th-Century Music

D. KERN HOLOMAN

University of California Press
Berkeley   Los Angeles   London

Copyright 1988
by D. Kern Holoman and
The Regents of the University of California

Library of Congress Cataloging-in-Publication Data

Main entry under title:
Writing about music.

1. Musical criticism—Authorship—Handbooks,
manuals, etc.   2. Music—Historiography—Handbooks,
manuals, etc.   3. Printing, Practical—Style manuals.
4. Music—Periodicals.   I. Holoman, D. Kern,
1947– 1. II. 19th-century music.
ML63.W68   1988   808'.06678   87–35693
ISBN 0-520-06382-1 (alk. paper)
Printed in the United States of America.
3 4 5 6 7 8 9

The paper used in this publication meets the minimum
requirements of American National Standard for Information Sciences—Permanence of Paper for Printed
Library Materials, ANSI Z39.48–1984. ∞

Contents

Introduction

Writing about music begins to be tricky, perhaps frustrating, the first time you try to reason out how to say Eroica Symphony in print. The rules for dealing with musical terminology are neither hard nor fast, and places where these are set forth with any system are few and far between. All good journals, however, keep style sheets on just these sorts of problems. What follows is a spruced-up, expanded version of the style sheet used by the editors and staff of the journal *19th-Century Music*, with virtually all the examples drawn from the pages of past issues of the magazine. The manner preferred by that arbiter of scholarly taste, the *Chicago Manual of Style* (13th edn., Chicago, 1982), is cited where applicable, and our deviations therefrom are noted.

Our style sheet was prepared from scratch, promulgated according to situations that actually cropped up, after discussions and occasional heated debate by our editors. We have changed our minds from time to time, and a few accommodations have been made to the new technologies of publication. But by and large we still believe in many of the principles to which we ascribed in the heady days of 1974 when we were dreaming the journal up.

We assembled the present pamphlet for a variety of reasons: first, in celebration of our tenth anniversary; second, because our editorial staff now spreads from sea to shining sea, and the original copy of the sheet has become exceeding dog-eared. We needed to have something a little more wieldy to argue over, and a document to send interested authors.

But we had, from the beginning, two other audiences equally in mind. The first was the university student, struggling to get his or her written assignment on music and music-making "right." I had referred students so often to *19th-Century Music* to see how thus-and-such an issue was handled that the office of the magazine was beginning to run short of back issues. Then there was the difficult problem any musician faces many times each year, that of preparing program copy. The attempt here is to address the needs of all three constituencies at once; you are cordially invited to skip over anything that does not pertain to your particular needs.

I have organized this pamphlet by beginning with some of the thorniest issues of discourse about music—namely, how we go about describing musical works and procedures in prose. Then I proceed to rules for dealing with the running narrative or expository text, a chapter on citations (i.e., notes and bibliography), and a treatment of such ancillary materials as musical examples, tables, and illustrations. There follow specialized chapters for concert producers and for authors desirous of submitting their work electronically. An Appendix contains an alphabetical list of words and situations that have given us pause.

19th-Century Music aims to maintain a graceful style that is similar from article to article within a single issue and consistent, if possible, from issue to issue. We favor a highly American style which we hope nevertheless manages to be acceptable internationally in its handling of the many languages and terminologies and formulations we regularly encounter. In our hope of encouraging high standards of literary expression, we have a (very short) list of words and formulas we try to deny: "such as," for example, and "utilize." We enjoy an occasional *da-da*, like our fondness for spelling "judgment" judgement. You will find all this below.

This style sheet is not intended to take the place of the standard works of reference on either music or writing. Student writers will wish to equip themselves with a good dictionary (we use a vintage Webster's *New Collegiate*, with occasional runs to *The American Heritage Dictionary*) and perhaps the *MLA Handbook for Writers of Research Papers* (2nd edn. New York, 1984), a publication that replaced the old *MLA Style Sheet* (1952, rev. edn. 1970). Probably you should invest in a paperback dictionary of music. (We use, in about equal measure, *The Concise Oxford Dictionary of Music* [3rd edn. London, 1980] and the *Harvard Concise Dictionary of Music* [Cambridge, Mass., 1978].) But first you must master *The Elements of Style*, a famous little pamphlet by William Strunk, Jr., and E. B. White (3rd edn. New York, 1979). Someday you may even wish to acquire your own copy of the *Chicago Manual of Style*, that Good Book which tells you all you may ever wish to know of publishers and publications. Finally, you will need to stay nearby a set of *The New Grove Dictionary of Music and Musicians* (6th edn. London, 1980)— though be careful of just *how* you use it; see 2.69, below.

For discussion of how the industry of musical discourse works, you may wish to read some or all of the following: "Music Publishing Today: A Symposium," *Notes* 32 (1975), 223–58 (see notably Claire

Brook's remarks, pp. 243–48); Michael Steinberg, "Introduction to Concerts in the Mass Media as a Means of Overcoming Cultural Barriers," in *International Musicological Society: Report of the Twelfth Congress, Berkeley, 1977*, ed. Daniel Heartz and Bonnie Wade (Kassel, 1981), pp. 550–69; D. Kern Holoman, "Publishing and/or Perishing," in *Musicology in the 1980s: Methods, Goals, Opportunities*, ed. D. Kern Holoman and Claude V. Palisca (New York, 1982), pp. 119–29.

The merits of the present booklet rest as much with the two other editors of *19th-Century Music*, Walter Frisch and Joseph Kerman, as they do with this author, and I must therefore commence these paragraphs of acknowledge[N.B.]ment with the deepest of thanks to this particular pair of cohorts through thick and thin. To the following go my equally sincere thanks. Tracey Rudnick helped assemble the materials for this revision of the style sheet, including most of the examples; Darin Wilson assisted in the late stages of readying the pamphlet for publication, and Jane-Ellen Long and Alain Hénon of the University of California Press shepherded it through production. Our tireless office staff have occupied themselves with these minutiae for many years. In Davis, these have been Christine Acosta, Kristi Brown, Donna M. Di Grazia, Nora McGuinness, and Cynthia Bates—names, if not faces, that will be familiar to all our authors. Joseph Kerman's assistants in Berkeley have included three fine musicologists who helped us forge the *19th-Century Music* style; these were Gary Tomlinson, Walter Frisch, and Patrick Macey. And two editors active in earlier periods of the magazine were instrumental in developing its philosophy and style; these were Robert Winter and Richard Swift.

On the subject of unfamiliar faces, I here salute with the most lasting of gratitude our typesetters and sometime technical advisers: the staff of the production department of A-R Editions, Inc., Madison, Wisconsin. In particular I thank the two ladies of vocal beauty at the other end of the telephone line, Donna Delaine and Mary Boss, for their unstinting, well, patience with us—a patience that's lasted now for the better part of a decade. Someday we shall make a deadline.

Style and consistency are ideals, and well-conceived ideals are usually difficult if not impossible to attain. There is nothing like promulgating rules for finding one's own mistakes. This little pamphlet is, therefore, dedicated to authors of today and tomorrow, forgetting the sins of the past with the toast of Liszt and the Futurists: *"A l'avenir!"*

DKH
Davis, California

1. Music Terminology

TITLES OF WORKS

1.1 Generally speaking there are formal and informal ways of calling a work. The formal title of a work from the classical repertoire always gives its genre or performing force, key, and index identifier.

1.2 *Generic Titles.* Generic titles are those, in English, that use such describers as symphony, concerto, fantasia, and the like, often with an identifying opus number or index number appended. These titles are given in roman type. Capitalization styles vary, but should be consistent throughout a work. At *19th-Century Music* we use the forms given below. (See also 1.15.)

> Bach: Toccata and Fugue in D Minor, BWV 565
> Haydn: Baryton Trio No. 71 in A Major, Hob. XI:71
> Beethoven: Violin Concerto in D Major, op. 61
> Beethoven's Fifth Symphony
> Schubert: Mass No. 6 in E♭ Major, D. 950
> Schumann: Variations for Piano, op. 9
> the Schumann Variations, op. 9
> Liszt: Piano Sonata in B Minor

1.3 True titles, i.e., those assigned by the composer, are given in italics. (For capitalization of foreign titles, see 2.43–48.)

> Bach: *Das Wohltemperierte Clavier*
> or, *The Well-Tempered Clavier*
> Beethoven: *Missa solemnis*
> Rossini: *La gazza ladra*
> Berlioz: *Symphonie fantastique*
> Mendelssohn: *Lieder ohne Worte*
> Verdi: *I masnadieri*
> Debussy: *La Mer*
> Stravinsky: *Le Sacre du printemps*
> Boulez: *Le Marteau sans maître*

1.4 *Common Names.* Many works are referred to by widely recognized popular names. These are generally put in quotation marks.

> Mozart: Symphony No. 41 in C Major ("Jupiter")

Beethoven: Piano Sonata No. 23 in F Minor, op. 57
  ("Appassionata")
Beethoven: Piano Trio in B♭ Major, op. 97 ("Archduke")
Schubert: Symphony No. 8 in B Minor ("Unfinished")
the "Archduke" Trio   the "Emperor" Concerto

To refer to Schubert's "Unfinished" Symphony may in a subtle way suggest that it really *isn't* unfinished at all, that the quotes are there as a sort of conspiratorial wink of the eye. There are, however, any number of unfinished symphonies of Schubert, but only one called the "Unfinished."

1.5   The rule of thumb is, then, that one italicizes the title that the composer himself gave to the work and puts common titles within quotation marks. These principles collide with vexing frequency; nicknames and true subtitles are often difficult to keep separate, and the matter of foreign languages complicates things still further. When in doubt, we almost invariably elect to use quotation marks.

> ("From the New World")   *Sonate Pathétique*
> the "New World" Symphony   the "Pathétique"
> the Pastoral Symphony
> the "Italian" Symphony

1.6   *Song Titles. 19th-Century Music* regards songs as full-fledged compositions, much as it regards doctoral dissertations as full-fledged books, and thus renders their titles in italic.

> *Der Leiermann (Winterreise)*   *Wohin?*
> *Meine Liebe ist grün*   *La danza*
> *Gretchen am Spinnrade*   *L'Heure exquise*

1.7   For a variety of reasons, however, we use roman type within quotation marks for arias drawn from operas.

> "Where'er You Walk," from Handel's *Semele*   "Porgi amor"

1.8   *Latin Liturgical Works.* Capitalize such titles as Mass, Requiem, and Te Deum, as well as their constituent movements; leave them in roman type.

> Kyrie   Gloria   Credo
> Sanctus   Agnus Dei   Benedictus

In view of the symbolic and structural function of these high sonorities in the Credo and Benedictus of the Mass, it is not surprising that Beethoven resorted to this framework again, in those parts of the choral finale of the Ninth Symphony with an explicitly religious text.

1.9 *Movement Titles.* These are capitalized and, in most cases, given in roman type.

We expect a string quartet to commence with a sonata-allegro movement, but to this point the Allegro has all the earmarks of an interjection within an Adagio movement.

1.10 Listings in concert programs and related publications require full formal titles. (See chapter 6.)

Beethoven: Concerto No. 4 for Piano and Orchestra in G Major, op. 58
Liszt: *Les Préludes* ("The Preludes"), Symphonic Poem after Lamartine

1.11 *Numbering of Symphonies by Schubert, Mendelssohn, and Dvořák.* These are especially difficult because more than one numbering system is or has been in wide use. We suggest the following, which reflect contemporary knowledge and practice and which are in each case the systems adopted by *The New Grove:*

Schubert:
Symphony No. 6 in C Major, D. 589 ("Little C-Major")
Symphony No. 7 in E Minor, D. 729 (a sketch)
Symphony No. 8 in B Minor, D. 759 ("Unfinished")
Symphony No. 9 in C Major, D. 944 ("Great C-Major")

Mendelssohn:
Symphony No. 3 in A Minor, op. 56 ("Scotch" or "Scottish")
Symphony No. 4 in A Major, op. 90 ("Italian")
Symphony No. 5 in D Major, op. 107 ("Reformation")

Dvořák:
Symphony No. 7 in D Minor, op. 70
Symphony No. 8 in G Major, op. 88
Symphony No. 9 in E Minor, op. 95 ("From the New World")

1.12 When an opus or catalogue number is used as sole identification of the work, it is not preceded by a comma.

Trio op. 97   Adagio K. 411

MAJOR AND MINOR

1.13 The words *major* and *minor* are identical in grammatical structure, both of them adjectives. The convention of upper-case Major and lower-case minor is correct only for some styles of chord notation, where such abbreviations as GM (G major) and Gm (G minor) can be quite useful.

> Sonata in A Major   Sonata in A Minor

1.14 When a key is used *preceding* a genre it becomes an adjectival construction and requires a hyphen.

> A-Major Sonata   A-Minor Sonata

CAPITALIZATION SCHEMES

1.15 See also 2.34–48. The following are typical examples:

> *Rhapsody in Blue*   *Bist du bei mir*
> *Ein deutsches Requiem*   *Ariettes oubliées*
> *Le Roi Lear*   *Prélude à "L'Après-midi d'un*
> *Les Vêpres siciliennes*   *faune"*
> *I vespri siciliani*   *Il re Lear*
>   *Il viaggio a Reims*

COMPOSERS' NAMES

1.16 Use transliterated, Americanized names for composers.

> Stravinsky   Scriabin   Dussek
> Tchaikovsky   Machaut   Josquin des Prez

1.17 *The Beethoven Problem.* According to the standard (Webster's) system, the name is broken "Bee - tho - ven." For those who are aware of the fact that *-hoven* is a common Dutch suffix, the only acceptable break must be "Beet - hoven." We have instructed our typesetter's computer to try to avoid the issue entirely, always separating the word as: "Beetho - ven."

1.18 *The Problem of Possessives.* There are any number of theories about the proper formation of possessives for names. We recommend that of the Chicago *Manual* (6.12–23): add an apostrophe *and* an *s*.

Berlioz's   Brahms's   Boulez's

One pronounces, incidentally, the *z* in Berlioz and Boulez.

1.19 *The Mendelssohn Problem.* Remember "Mendel's son" in this most frequently misspelled of composers' names.

Mendels - sohn

1.20 *The Russian Problem.* Transliteration from the Russian alphabet is, at best, a vexing problem; see 2.60–61. We have adopted the spellings given in 1.23. Note especially:

Rachmaninov   Stravinsky   Tchaikovsky

1.21 *The Schoenberg Problem.* Schoenberg dropped the umlaut when he immigrated to the United States. In virtually every circumstance, English authors should use:

Schoenberg

1.22 *Names with "von."* By and large the *von* is omitted, except in the full name.

Dittersdorf   Gluck   Weber

but usually:

von Bülow

1.23 *Summary.* The following is a list of names that have posed difficulties of one sort or another to the editors of *19th-Century Music*, with their hyphenations:

Bach, Carl Phi - lipp Ema - nu - el	De - bus - sy
Bar - tók, Bé - la	De - libes
Beet - ho - ven	De - lius
Ber - lioz	Di - a - ghi - lev
Bi - zet	D'In - dy (upper-case *D*)
Bo - ro - din	Du - kas
Brahms	Dvo - řák
Bruck - ner	Fau - ré
Cho - pin, Fré - dé - ric	Franck
Cle - men - ti	Glin - ka

Gou - nod	Rim - sky – Kor - sa - kov
Grieg	Ros - si - ni
Hof - manns - thal	Schoen - berg
Ja - ná - ček	Schu - bert
Kre - nek	Schu - mann
Liszt	Scri - a - bin, Alex - an - der
Mah - ler	Sme - ta - na
Men - dels - sohn	Strauss
Mo - zart	Stra - vin - sky
Mus - sorg - sky	Tchai - kov - sky
Pa - ga - ni - ni	Ver - di
Prač (not Pratsch)	von Bü - low
Rach - ma - ni - nov	Wag - ner
Ra - vel	We - ber
Re-spi-ghi	

1.24 *Other Difficult Names in Music Study.*

Réti (the theorist, with his accent)	Shake - speare, Shakespearean
Virgil	Theodor Adorno

THEMATIC CATALOGUES OF COMPOSERS' WORKS

1.25 Thematic catalogues are abbreviated with a letter or letters suggesting the author's name, followed by a period.

K. 191	In Köchel's catalogue of Mozart, the Bassoon Concerto in B♭ Major
D. 628	In Deutsch's catalogue of Schubert, *Erlkönig*
J. 277	In Jahn's catalogue of Weber, *Der Freischütz*
Hob. XXII:9	In Hoboken's catalogue of Haydn, the *Missa in tempore belli*

1.26 The exception is BWV, for *Bach-Werke-Verzeichnis,* Wolfgang Schmieder's catalogue of the works of Bach. This is usually abbreviated without periods.

BWV 1050	In the *Bach-Werke-Verzeichnis,* the Fifth Brandenburg Concerto

PITCH NAMES

1.27 For most purposes a simple upper-case letter defines pitch names well enough.

The high C immediately descends two octaves and loses every trace of energy.

The bass moves sequentially from G to B♭ to D.

1.28 The plural of a pitch name takes simply an *s*, not *'s*.

Its symmetrical images (m. 7: the Cs) are now stable and dramatically executed.

1.29 When octave register must be specified, we prefer the system that calls the C two octaves below middle C "Great C."

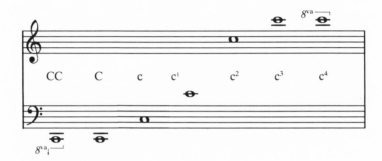

In mm. 96–97, only g^2 in the right hand and g^1 in the left are to be brought out with a *forte*; the immediately adjacent $a♭^2$ and $a♭^1$ are already to be played *piano*.

1.30 When a series of pitches is given, join the pitch names with *en*-dashes (see 2.28).

The initial F–G–F–B♭ provides the framework for the vocal phrase that begins songs 3, 5, and 7.

DYNAMICS

1.31 Directions for dynamic nuance are given in italic.

piano, pianissimo	*mezzo piano, mezzo forte*
forte, fortissimo	*sforzando*

Returning to the *pianissimo* level, it reinterprets the B as an element of a normal V^7.

The Horowitz recording shows an astonishing control of dynamics through a myriad of levels between *pianissimo* and *mezzo forte*.

1.32 Abbreviations of these terms for dynamic nuance may be in italic as well. *19th-Century Music* prefers to use boldface italic, for clarity.

The movement originally ended *ff* at what is now m. 493.

NUMBERS

1.33 *Meter Signatures.* These are given in roman or boldface roman characters. Set the constituents of a numerical meter signature directly over each other, not as a fraction.

The one is in major and **C** ($\frac{4}{2}$), and the other is in minor and $\frac{2}{4}$.

1.34 *Figured-Bass Symbols.* These are quite small, since two and sometimes three of them must fit within a line of type. Take care to specify the exact position of the sharps and flats, so as not to confuse D♭ ^{7} with D$^{♭7}$.

The second chord of ex. 3 is $\frac{7}{5}$ on the dominant.

The first movement opens with a bold, terse gesture, a I$^6_4$–V^{13}–I cadence which echoes down the whole length of the exposition and development.

1.35 *Pitch-Class Symbols.* The caret-over-the-Arabic-numeral as an indication of pitch-class is a designation we try to avoid simply because of the difficulty many typesetting systems have in setting the carets squarely over Arabic numerals. Sometimes, however, the carets are essential to the thrust of the discussion.

In mm. 229–33 the rising fourths, which had always been left open ($\hat{1}$–$\hat{4}$ / $\hat{2}$–$\hat{5}$) are closed ($\hat{1}$–$\hat{4}$ / $\hat{5}$–$\hat{1}$).

The "sigh" motive is now identified with the neighboring motion ♭$\hat{6}$–$\hat{5}$ (G♭–F) or $\hat{6}$–$\hat{5}$ (G–F), the local representative in B♭ major of the C♭–C conflict (i.e., ♭$\hat{6}$ and ♮$\hat{6}$ in E♭ major).

1.36 Rehearsal numbers are generally given in boxes, especially since we discovered how fond computers are of drawing boxes.

The Adagietto at ⬚52 is centered on D and carries a signature of two sharps, while the music from ⬚54 to ⬚58 has E at its center.

OTHER

1.37 On the question of italic or roman typeface for such musical terminology as "pizzicato" and "tremolo," see 2.87–89, 93. Roman is generally preferable.

1.38 Pitches reside on a *staff* (sing.) or *staves* (pl.).

> manuscript paper of thirty-two staves
> twelve-staff paper
> the crosshatching in staff 8

2. Narrative Text

NUMBERS

2.1   Spell out numbers under 100.

> The membership of forty was comprised of fourteen painters, eight sculptors, eight architects, four engravers, and six composers.

2.2   Use Arabic numerals for most numbers over 100.

> Before the eighteenth century was over, some 150 Russian comic operas had been written and performed.

2.3   *But* do not begin a sentence with a numeral.

> Two hundred pages of music paper devoted to two-staff sketches for the Great C-Major Symphony would have seemed like an ample initial supply.

2.4   In some circumstances "a hundred" is preferable to "100," "a thousand" to "1,000," and so on.

> On his return, Professor Holoman had to write *jejune* a hundred times on his office blackboard.

2.5   For *19th-Century Music*, a completed series takes the last two digits of the completing number. Note the use of *en*-dashes. (Chicago *Manual* style is given in parentheses.)

> | | | |
> |---|---|---|
> | 22–37 | 200–08 (200–208) | 1756–91 |
> | 122–27 | 1003–09 (1003–9) | 1803–69 |

2.6   Hyphenate adjectival forms.

> twenty-four-year-old man   8^1/$_2$-x-11-inch paper

DATES

2.7 For full dates, give day, then month, then year. This system is both logical and in wide use internationally.

> 17 June 1882

2.8 Do not separate out the year with commas.

> October 1954
>
> As late as December 1822, we find him piqued by assertions that the success of *Freischütz* depended chiefly on the "Teufelspark" in the work.

2.9 A span of time is best expressed as follows, using an *en*-dash.

> 9–18 August 1881   1770–1827   1840–93

2.10 *Decades.* We—*pace* Chicago *Manual*—use Arabic numbers for decades, without an apostrophe.

> the 1850s   the early 80s

2.11 For pairs of decades, though our practice has varied, we now generally use no punctuation:

> the 1850s and 60s

2.12 *Centuries.* Spell out centuries.

> the nineteenth century

2.13 Hyphenate adjectival forms (see 2.6).

> nineteenth-century opera

The correct linear title of our journal is thus *19th-Century Music*. Only in the logotype do we drop the hyphen. We prefer, incidentally, the abbreviation *NCM*.

2.14 *Russian Dates.* By and large, convert dates to the modern Gregorian system. When the old system is to be distinguished from the new system, use the abbreviations O.S. and N.S.

> Berlioz's first St. Petersburg concert was on 28 November 1867 (N.S.; 16 November, O.S., and not the 17th, as alleged by Husson).

In the nineteenth century the N.S. dates are twelve days later than those in the Old System.

2.15 *French Republican Calendar.* A date from the picturesque calendar developed for the First Republic is correctly given as follows, with its conversion into the ordinary Gregorian calendar.

> *le 9 Thermidor, an II de la République* (27 July 1794)

The usual treatment is something along the following lines:

> This was the Convention of 26 Messidor, year IX (15 July 1801), promulgated on 18 Germinal, year X (8 April 1802).

MONEY

2.16 *American Money.* In running text, American money is given in Arabic numbers preceded by the dollar sign.

> $1.00 (not $1) $.50 (no space, not 50¢) $1 million

2.17 *Foreign Currencies.* These are expressed as follows:

> £   (British pounds sterling)   FF   (French francs)
> LIT   (Italian lire)   FB   (Belgian francs)
> DM   (German marks)   FS   (Swiss francs)

SIMPLE PUNCTUATION

2.18 *Series Commas.* Use a comma before the final *and.*

> The men were disguised as a devil, a pig, a goat, and a woman.

2.19 *Periods.* The period goes within the parentheses only if what is within is a complete sentence—in which case it must begin with a capital letter.

> (*Freischütz* had been given in Petersburg in 1824 and reached Moscow the following year.)

> Julian Coates, the hero of Harris's new novel *Tenth,* is in fact the kind of musicologist one can easily admire—not for his academic place (he teaches lower-level courses at a Southern California college), nor for his publications (he seems only to have an article in a journal called *Music World*), nor for his attractive personality and rather enviable sex life, nor because he manages with inspired skill to complete Adrian Leverkühn's Tenth Symphony,

. . . not for any of this, but because he figures so prominently in a novel that's not only elegantly written but informed by insight both literary and musical (a reference to the academic subject of music "harmonics" notwithstanding).

2.20 The Chicago *Manual* demands that the period be placed inside all quotation marks, but we find it more legible to place the period between the inner and the outer quotation mark.

> "Through these repetitions, societies act 'to regenerate themselves periodically'."

2.21 The mark of punctuation within the quotation marks is considered to end the sentence, except when the quotation marks are followed by an end parenthesis.

> The first section of the Adagio brings a drop in register, a shift motivated by the text: "Ihr stürzt nieder, Millionen?" ("Do you fall on your knees, millions?").

2.22 *Abbreviations Using Two Periods.* These are separated by a space only when they are personal initials.

e.g.,	n.d. (no date)
i.e.,	n.p., n.d. (no place, no date)
Englewood Cliffs, N.J.	Ph.D.
Garden City, N.Y.	O.S. / N.S. (Russian calendar)

but

J. B. Loeillet	T. S. Eliot

2.23 *Colons and Semicolons.* They are almost invariably placed outside quotation marks and parentheses.

> In the Requiem this is the notorious thirty-six-measure pedal on D, the foundation for the fugue "Der Gerechten Seelen sind in Gottes Hand"; in the rondo the coda contains . . .

ELLIPSES

2.24 No mark of punctuation seems to confuse authors more than the ellipsis, a series of *three* dots, separated by spaces, to indicate an omission in the quotation.

> The newspapers and periodicals are . . . the national history at its most self-conscious.

2.25 Before the ellipsis often comes the mark of punctuation the context requires. Thus there will often be a series of *four* dots: the period plus the three dots of the ellipsis.

> Music, art, charity, and society met with a great loss in the absence of Mr. Meiggs. The Music Hall . . . was built by that gentleman. . . . Many celebrities came to California by the influence of Mr. Meiggs.

2.26 Since quotations are almost invariably preceded and succeeded by non-quoted material, marks of ellipsis are generally superfluous at the beginning and end of quotations.

2.27 The exception to this rule occurs when a cited sentence or thought is begun in midstream or somehow left dangling.

> Words like—
> " . . . Beneath the roof of quiet night?
> How slowly passed the tedious day!
> How slowly the glow of evening died away!"
> —are out of place and unsuited to music.

DASHES

2.28 Note the difference between the *em*-dash, typed -- and printed —, and the *en*-dash, typed - (or, better, = -) and printed –. The *em*-dash is the conventional mark of punctuation for overall sentence structure; the *en*-dash is used principally to connect series of numbers.

> This remark, if authentic—and one hopes it is—referred to Schenker's earliest published writings.

> Neither the autograph draft of the program (April–May 1830) nor its publication in *Le Figaro* on 21 May 1830 contains any references to the concluding events of the movement.

2.29 Use the *en*-dash to connect dates, pages, pitches, and keys, and in a compound adjective of which one element contains a hyphen or consists of two words.

19–21 May	the D♭–D♮–D♭–C figure
the famous 1827–28 season	G major–G minor–G major
pp. 327–72	W. S. Gilbert–style verse
mm. 36–40	pitch-class–number notation

QUOTATION MARKS

2.30 Virtually all quotation marks used by *19th-Century Music* are given in roman type, which is usually more legible.

2.31 But quotation marks *within* a passage in italic are also italic.

> The material from which Jonas compiled his *Entwurf einer "Lehre vom Vortrag"* probably dates from various periods in Schenker's life.

2.32 *19th-Century Music* has abandoned its former policy of putting quotations from foreign languages in both italic type and quotation marks and in most cases now gives priority to the quotation marks.

SUPERSCRIPT NOTE NUMBERS

2.33 With very few exceptions, superscript note numbers go outside a mark of punctuation. Where at all possible, they should come at the end of a complete sentence.

> As he inimitably put it: "I resigned as a nice organist and gave up music."[9]
>
> Mazzini could appeal to music to develop a social and a political conscience as well as an artistic one;[160] . . .
>
> (For a summary list by category, see table 2.[22])

This last is contrary to Chicago *Manual* 15.39, but we think it looks better.

CAPITALIZATION

2.34 In general, use lower-case letters in preference to upper-case.

> chapter 3   figure 3   act II, sc. 3

2.35 *Sections of Sonata Form.* In general, names of sections of the sonata form speak for themselves, without the necessity of an upper-case letter to start.

> exposition   development   recapitulation

2.36 *Genres.* By the same token, nouns of genre work well in lower-case.

<blockquote>

symphony	the *Tristan* prelude
minuet and trio	In the overture to *La gazza ladra* . . .

</blockquote>

2.37 *Periods of Music History.* The commonly used periods of music history are capitalized, both as nouns and, with the exception of the word *medieval*, as adjectives.

<blockquote>

the Renaissance	the Classical Style	Romanticism
the Baroque	the Romantic Period	Impressionism

</blockquote>

and by extension:

<blockquote>

the Enlightenment	a medieval mystery play
the Second Empire	the Renaissance madrigal
the Baroque violin	the Classical symphony

</blockquote>

2.38 Lower-case is appropriate for *classical* and *romantic* when used to suggest attitude or philosophical orientation.

> Though a product of this romantic attachment, the work has a classical elegance of design.

2.39 *German Nouns.* Take care to capitalize these.

<blockquote>

Lied, Lieder	Ländler

</blockquote>

2.40 *Titles of Musical Works.* See 1.1–12, 2.36, 2.43, and 2.48.

2.41 *Summary Table of Words Not Capitalized.*

<blockquote>

chapter 3 (ch. 3)	ms., mss.
diagram 1	opus, op.
example 3 (ex. 3)	plate 1
figure 2 (fig. 2)	scene 2
folio 28 (fol. 28)	stanza 4
medieval	table 1

</blockquote>

2.42 *Summary Table of Words Capitalized.*

<blockquote>

Baroque	Lied, Lieder
Classical	the Middle Ages
the Enlightenment	Renaissance
Ländler	Romantic, Romanticism

</blockquote>

CAPITALIZATION SCHEMES IN FOREIGN LANGUAGES

2.43 *French.* Capitalize *titles* through the first noun or proper noun.

L'Enfant prodigue	*La Bonne Chanson*
Rapsodie espagnole	*Grande Messe des morts*
Grande Symphonie funèbre et triomphale	

2.44 It is elegant to capitalize a pair of nouns, especially in titles of periodicals.

Revue et Gazette musicale   *Journal des Débats*

2.45 Because they are always given in roman typeface, and thus otherwise might confuse the context if done according to the rules above, all constituents of organizations and institutions should be capitalized according to English rules.

Bibliothèque Nationale
Association des Artistes Musiciens
Société des Concerts du Conservatoire
Société Nationale des Chemins-de-Fer

2.46 *19th-Century Music* has usually hyphenated names of theaters with a lower-case letter following the hyphen.

Opéra-comique   Théâtre-italien   Comédie-française

2.47 Place-names are usually joined with hyphens, particularly when they are based on names of the saints.

St.-Jean-de-Luz	rue St.-André-des-Arts
St.-Juan-les-Pins	place St.-Michel
La Côte-St.-André	place Igor-Stravinsky

Note the use of lower-case for *rue* and *place*.

2.48 *Italian.* Capitalize only the first letter of a title.

Così fan tutte   *La gazza ladra*

DIACRITICS

2.49 Decent type fonts include diacritics and special characters for most European languages. These should be carefully specified in texts cited from foreign languages.

2.50 Use accents on capitals as well as lower-case characters (except for the French preposition *A*). Take particular care to specify these clearly in the manuscript, as it is a commonly held but erroneous belief among authors that upper-case letters require no accents.

> *Édouard Bénazet*   *La Fuite en Égypte*

2.51 When quoting passages from foreign languages in a typescript, take care to note occurrences of characters not available on conventional American keyboards, notably ß.

> Weber's *Große Oper:* A Note on the Origins of *Euryanthe*

2.52 *Diacritics in Borrowed English.* These are all given in roman type, with preference generally given to retaining the accent.

> dénouement   étude   précis
> à propos   résumé

2.53 *Borrowings without Diacritics.* Omit the diacritic only for foreign words *firmly* established in American usage.

> debut   elite   naive
> premiere   role

LIGATURES

2.54 Ligatures may be omitted from Latin and Greek.

> Dies irae   *Encyclopaedia Britannica*

2.55 Most typesetting systems, including that used by *19th-Century Music,* provide the modern French ligature œ.

> œuvre   *but:* hors d'oeuvre

2.56 After some years of floundering, we have adopted the following spelling, always:

> aesthetic

WORD BREAKS

2.57 In virtually every European language but English, the word break is between consonants or after the vowel and before the consonant—but the first and last syllables must contain more than one letter each.

> *Tu - ran - dot*   *Zau - ber - flöte*   *Tro - va - to - re*

Algorithms in most American word-processing systems favor, of course, American practice, so it is important to keep this matter in mind when reading proofs containing material in foreign languages.

2.58 German compound words break first into their components; thus, the word may *not* break between doubled letters that end one component.

> Gott - heit   Bassett - horn

but

> Abend - dämmerung

2.59 In general, follow the instructions in the Chicago *Manual* 6.33–47. Because *19th-Century Music* is set in two narrow columns, the matter of word breaks is especially troublesome, and there is sometimes lexicographical disagreement over the proper separation. For example, the word "performance" is separated "per - form - ance" in the dictionary in my office and "per - for - mance" in the dictionary downstairs in the magazine office, both of them Webster's. (It took us a heated, accusatory half-hour to figure this out.) The current standard is that of *Webster's Ninth New Collegiate Dictionary* (Springfield, Mass., 1985), which gives "per - for - mance."

RUSSIAN

2.60 In general *19th-Century Music* endeavors to follow the precepts of the Chicago *Manual* 9.86–101 on Russian, transliterating into the Latin alphabet roughly according to the systems of the United States Board on Geographic Names and the Library of Congress. Some examples follow.

> "Ne tomi, rodimyi" ("Grieve not, beloved")
> *Sobranie narodnykh russkikh pesen*
> muzhik

                                                    Russkaia muzyka
                                                    fantaziia-shutka

2.61 Give translations of Russian titles in parentheses and quotation marks.

> *Kto brat, kto sestra* ("Brother or Sister?")
> *Babushkiny popugai* ("Grandma's Parrots")
> "Vniz po natushke po Volge" ("Down by Mother Volga")

BRITISHISMS

2.62 Britishisms are to be avoided in nearly every case.

2.63 Avoid *-our* spellings.

> *not:* colour   endeavour   honours

2.64 Avoid *-ise* spellings.

> *not:* emphasise   harmonise   organise

2.65 Avoid precious British constructs.

> *not:* amongst   thrice   club together

2.66 Avoid British music terminology.

> *not:* gramophone   crotchet   quaver

2.67 Avoid anglicized place-names.

> *not* Lyons *but* Lyon
> *not* Marseilles *but* Marseille
> *not* Leghorn *but* Livorno

2.68 In an exception to this rule, we *do* use the following:

> acknowledgement   judgement

This is because we hold, doubtless naively, that the principal advantage of American English is that things are spelled as they sound. One pleasure of editing a magazine is the privilege of making up one's own rules.

A "Reader in Favor of American Spelling" wrote to us as follows:

> I always enjoy reading *19th-Century Music,* but why do you insist on spelling "judgment" *judgement?* Coping with this is similar to reading misspellings in a term paper.

We responded:

> Our admittedly idiosyncratic view is that American English should look, as much as possible, like it sounds; "judgment" looks to us like it should be pronounced *jugment*. (We try also to use "acknowledgement.") We doubt our reader will look upon this explanation with much favour.

2.69 *Note for Student Writers.* You must enjoy *The New Grove*, which is a monument of English-speaking scholarship. With its picturesque spines (Back to Bolivia, Jacobus to Kerman, Mūwashaḥ to Ory, Spiridion to Tin Whistle), overall high quality of historical and critical writing, and handsome illustrations (even including the upside-down-and-backwards facsimile of a Wagner autograph, vol. 20, p. 126), *Grove* is fascinating wherever you open it up. But younger writers should be especially careful not to absorb the Britishisms they will find there.

ABBREVIATIONS

2.70 The following abbreviations are used almost invariably:

ca.	circa	no.	number (nos., numbers)
cm.	centimeter	op.	opus (op. 59, no. 1)
m.	measure (mm., measures)	ops.	opuses, opera (also opp.)
n.	note or footnote (p. 60n)	rpt.	reprint, reprinted, reprinted by

2.71 The following are used according to context, with the abbreviation used if possible:

ch.	chapter	l., ll.	line, lines
ed.	editor (eds., editors), edited by	rev.	revision, revised, revised by
edn.	edition	sc.	scene
ex(s).	example, examples	trans.	translation, translated by
facs.	facsimile	vol(s).	volume, volumes

2.72 *Latin Abbreviations.* The Latin abbreviations for *exempli gratia* and *id est* are given in roman type, have no space, and are invariably followed by a comma. These are lower-case except at the beginning of a sentence.

e.g.,	(*exempli gratia;* for example)
i.e.,	(*id est;* that is)

2.73 *French Abbreviations.* To avoid confusing *M* for Monsieur and *M.* for Marcel, omit the period after the abbreviations for Monsieur, Madame, and so forth.

> M, MM   Monsieur, Messieurs
> Mme, Mmes   Madame, Mesdames
> Mlle, Mlles Mademoiselle, Mesdemoiselles

2.74 *Abbreviations for Thematic Catalogues.* See 1.25–26.

BLOCK CITATIONS

2.75 Quotations and illustrative material longer than two or three lines of running text is presented in the form of a block citation, in reduced typesize and without quotation marks. These should remain *double-spaced* in typescripts and be indicated by indentation left and right.

2.76 Lists and other illustrative devices often look and read better when given as block citations.

> Using "illustration" as a generic term, Kivy identifies seven types of musical illustration. Musical *pictures* constitute two of them:
>> 1. Pieces of music that sound like something else (the subject of representation) where the "subject will be immediately and universally identified . . . without any verbal (or other) aids" (e.g., *Pacific 231*) and
>> 2. Pieces that sound like something else where identification of the subject requires the "minimal information" (p. 35) that the piece is an illustration (e.g., the thunderstorm in Beethoven's Sixth Symphony).
> The other five types are cases of non-pictorial representation.

2.77 *19th-Century Music* distinguishes between running-text block citations, which are given reduced typesize but not indented, and block citations of poetry, which are indented with the usual line-breaks. A third category includes libretti with character names, where our format involves a tab-stop:

> LEAR: (*con tutta l'anima*)
>   Addoppia o Cielo i fulmini
>   Fa d'orni ingrato cenere.
> KENT: (*a lui*) Deh nell'umil tugurio
>   Il capo tuo ricovera.

REFERENCES IN RUNNING TEXT

2.78 References to musical examples are abbreviated, except when the word *example* or *figure* falls at the beginning of the sentence.

> The motive appears in a kind of inchoate state, identifiable by its major-sixth *initium,* but minus its falling-fourth cadence (ex. 5).
>
> Example 5 comes from op. 41, no. 104, dated 27 March 1893.

2.79 In most situations, reference to an act-and-scene of an opera or theater work is best abbreviated.

> The next exchange between the lovers occurs in act II, sc. 4 ("D'un uom che geme").

2.80 *Page References in Running Text.* For main-text quotation, simply put the page number outside the closing quotation mark and before the period.

> "We know, however, that Schubert had purchased almost a hundred additional leaves of TYPE III paper before departing Vienna" (p. 232).

2.81 For block quotations, our practice has varied widely, largely out of my own aversion to a reference as follows:

> All other music, though a joy, was merely sound. (p. 12)

The problem here is a "sentence" that begins with a lower-case letter and has no period. Yet *(P. 12.)* looks silly and *(Page 12.)* is unwieldy. Of late we have adopted the following:

> But saddest of all was a song my mother sometimes sang as prepayment for taking a nap. It was "Darling Nelly Grey," and I could never listen to the end without tears in my throat. All other music, though a joy, was merely sound (p. 12).

ROMAN AND ITALIC

2.82 In general use roman type in preference to italic.

2.83 Punctuation following a word is always in the typeface of the word preceding.

> Of all the movements of the *Missa solemnis,* none is more copiously documented in Beethoven's sketchbooks than the Credo.

2.84 Quotation marks are nearly always roman; see 2.30–32.

2.85 Parentheses are nearly always roman.

> The *dramatis personae* reflects the final discussions: Lear, his three daughters, Edmondo Duca di Glocester, Mica (*il buffone di Lear*), Giorgio Conte di Kent . . .

2.86 We do, however, rely heavily on italic typeface for single words borrowed from foreign languages.

> Scene 2: the *scena ultima* in prison.
>
> Verdi was, of course, writing for a stage that required a *mise-en-scène* that was, by Elizabethan standards, very elaborate: massive dropcloths, *laterali*, and substantial properties. He was obliged to think in terms of a small number of large scenic *mutazioni*, precisely as did producers of elaborate Shakespearean plays in the late nineteenth and early twentieth centuries.

2.87 Such words as crescendo, pizzicato, ostinato, legato, ritornello are best left in roman, recognizing their universal usage.

2.88 The exceptions are usually subtle quotations.

> Then he went back and added the direction *pizzicato*.

2.89 Words usually given in italic include:

> *a cappella*   *da capo*   *gratis*

2.90 *Sic* is usually given, for emphasis, in the opposite typeface from the quotation in which it is found. It is virtually always enclosed in square brackets.

> [Mendelssohn, writing in English:] I think if any, this must way lead [*sic*] to an improvement of the taste of the public, as well as the professors, and every lover of music must feel interested in such an undertaking.

2.91 Single letters go in italic.

> Hors d'oeuvre has no *s* at the end.

2.92 *Summary Table of Words Usually Given in Italic.*

> *a cappella*   *forte*   *œuvre*
> *da capo*   *fortissimo*   *piano*

2.93 *Summary Table of Words Usually Given in Roman.*

allargando	obbligato
avant garde	op. cit.
bona fide	ostinato
dénouement	per se
"Eroica"	pizzicato
fermata	précis
finale	prima donna
ibid.	pseud.
legato	ritard.
Leitmotiv	ritornello
libretti	tremolo
Lied, Lieder	tutti

OTHER *19th-CENTURY MUSIC* HOUSE RULES

2.94 Generally, omit doubled letters where both spellings are encountered.

canceled	modeled	penciled
focused	traveled	

2.95 *-ly* constructions are always open (i.e., without hyphen).

a frequently cited source

2.96 Omit the *s* from:

toward	afterward

2.97 Do not begin a sentence with *However.*

2.98 Spell *theater* with *er.*

2.99 Avoid, where possible, the use of:

such as	utilize

2.100 Hyphenate after *mid* only when it is an adjective.

Realism had great strengths in France at mid century.
a mid-century *romance*

FORMAT AND DESIGN

2.101 Shortish paragraphs are preferred over very long ones.

2.102 *Subdivisions.* Subdivisions of long articles are encouraged by *19th-Century Music* and may be accomplished by double line-space between paragraphs, by double line-space with roman numeral on a separate line, or by double line-space with subheading on a separate line.

2.103 We strongly frown on digressive sentences in parentheses, preferring instead the *em*-dash.

> A musical pun of sorts is at work here—Chopin reverts to it elsewhere in the Preludes—that conceives of a technical supertonic sonority as an intensified submediant.

FINALLY . . .

2.104 *All manuscript* destined for the attention of editors or typesetters must be *double-spaced:* notes, captions, bibliography—everything!

2.105 With virtually no exceptions, sentences begin with upper-case letters and conclude with a mark of punctuation, usually the period.

2.106 Use of italics and exclamation points for emphasis is effective only when kept to a minimum.

3. Citations

3.1 Citations (notes, bibliography) endeavor to present publication data on sources used, in order, first, to give appropriate credit to research and critical work done by others and, second, to refer the reader to sources for further consultation.

3.2 A bibliography of works cited may be given at the end of an academic publication. Such a bibliography is usually arranged in alphabetical order by author's surname; it is sometimes subdivided into categories (books, articles, scores). True bibliographies are uncommon in articles for scholarly journals; for further discussion of these, see Chicago *Manual*, chapter 16. For most paper- or article-length writing about music you should follow the abbreviated style of citation used in *19th-Century Music*. Some examples follow.

ARTICLES

3.3 *Articles from* The New Grove:

> Arthur Hedley, Maurice J. E. Brown, and Nicholas Temperley, "Chopin, Fryderyk Franciszek," *The New Grove Dictionary of Music and Musicians*, ed. Stanley Sadie (London, 1980), vol. 4, pp. 292–307.

3.4 *Articles from Learned Journals:*

> William Kinderman, "Beethoven's Symbol for the Deity in the *Missa solemnis* and the Ninth Symphony," *19th-Century Music* 9 (1985), 102–18.

Often a colon is used between the date and the page numbers.

> (1985): 102–18.

3.5 We do not abbreviate titles of journals, but we often simplify them.

> this journal (for *19th-Century Music*)

Journal of the American Musicological Society (not *JAMS*)
Musical Quarterly (not *The Musical Quarterly*)
Musical Times (not *The Musical Times*)
Music & Letters (not *Music and Letters*)
Notes (not *MLA Notes*)

3.6 *Articles from Book-Length Collections of Essays* (including Festschriften). This is the only situation where we ordinarily use the word "in."

> Karl-Heinz Köhler, "The Conversation Books: Aspects of a New Picture of Beethoven," in *Beethoven, Performers, and Critics*, ed. Robert Winter and Bruce Carr (Detroit, 1980), pp. 147–61.
>
> Edward T. Cone, "Bach's Unfinished Fugue in C Minor," in *Studies in Renaissance and Baroque Music in Honor of Arthur Mendel*, ed. Robert L. Marshall (Kassel and Hackensack, N.J., 1974), pp. 149–55.

BOOKS

3.7 The standard book citation is as follows:

> David Charlton, *Grétry and the Growth of Opéra-Comique* (Cambridge, 1986).
>
> Winton Dean, *Bizet* (rev. edn. London, 1975).

3.8 Note the use of place and date without publisher, as is common in the field of music study. When the publisher is named, use a colon.

> References throughout are to the original Ricordi publication of the full score (Milan, 1893), which has recently been issued in a photo-reprint (New York: Dover Publications, 1980).

3.9 A colon separates the title from the subtitle.

> *Ton und Wort: The Lieder of Richard Strauss.*
> *Nineteenth-Century Music Manuscripts in The Pierpont Morgan: A Checklist.*

3.10 Note that the University of California Press prefers place names of both places of publication.

> Douglas Johnson, Alan Tyson, and Robert Winter, *The Beethoven Sketchbooks* (Berkeley and Los Angeles, 1985).

3.11 Use "Cambridge" to mean the seat of Cambridge University Press; "Cambridge, Mass." as the seat of Harvard University Press and MIT Press.

3.12 *Multi-Volume Works.* When all volumes of a multi-volume work or collection appeared simultaneously, the following style is used in *19th-Century Music*.

> Theodore Henry Hittell, *History of California* (San Francisco, 1897), III, 434–41.
>
> Richard Graf du Moulin Eckart, *Cosima Wagner, ein Lebens- und Charakterbild* (Munich, 1929), I, 9–10.

Note that this is virtually the only use of roman numerals in citations in our journal.

3.13 It is not strictly necessary and is often redundant to specify how many volumes are included in a multi-volume set, but occasionally this is helpful information.

> *The Wellesley Guide to Victorian Periodicals,* ed. Walter Edwards Houghton, 3 vols. (Toronto, 1966–); a fourth volume is projected.
>
> August Göllerich and Max Auer, *Anton Bruckner: Ein Lebens- und Schaffensbild,* 4 vols. in 9 (Regensburg, 1922–37), 3/1 (1932), p. 226.

3.14 When the volumes appeared at different times, put place and date of publication after volume number. Give the volume number as a roman numeral preceded by the abbreviation *vol.*

> Brahms, *Briefwechsel,* vol. V (Berlin, 1921), p. 31.

3.15 Note that the practice of some series is to give Arabic numbers to volumes. Among the most frequently cited of these are *The New Grove* and the New Berlioz Edition.

> See the facsimile given by Jürgen Kindermann in his edn. of the Requiem, New Berlioz Edition, vol. 9 (Kassel, 1978), p. 159.

3.16 *Editors.* Use the abbreviation *ed.* The name of the editor comes *after* the title:

> Honoré de Balzac, *Lettres à Mme Hanska,* ed. Roger Pierrot (Paris, 1967).

3.17 *Subsequent editions.* Although it is not common practice, for clarity's sake *19th-Century Music* uses the abbreviation *edn.* for "edition" and does not use a comma before the data on publication.

> Donald Jay Grout, *A Short History of Opera* (2nd edn. New York, 1965).
>
> Philippe Fauré-Fremit, *Gabriel Fauré* (Paris, 1929; 2nd edn. 1957).

3.18 It is useful to the reader to be informed of the existence of reprints. Use the abbreviation *rpt.*

> J. A. Westrup, "The Chamber Music," in *Music of Schubert*, ed. Gerald Abraham (1947; rpt. Port Washington, N.Y., 1969), p. 93.
>
> "Vom Organischen der Sonatenform," in *Das Meisterwerk in der Musik* 2 (Munich, etc., 1926; rpt. Hildesheim, 1974), p. 51 (translation mine). A translation of the complete essay, by Orin Grossman, appeared as "Organic Structure in Sonata Form," in *Readings in Schenker Analysis and Other Approaches*, ed. Maury Yeston (New Haven, 1977), pp. 38–53.

OTHER

3.19 *Dissertations.* We grant the Ph.D. dissertation the status of a book by listing it in italics. Simply specify *Ph.D. diss.*, university, and date.

> Linda Correll Roesner, *Studies in Schumann Manuscripts* (Ph.D. diss., New York University, 1973).

3.20 *Newspapers.* Give the date and the page numbers.

> *Broadway Journal*, 27 September 1845, pp. 180–83.

3.21 *Publishers' Series.* It is sometimes useful and occasionally mandatory to specify these.

> Berchet, *Opere*, vol. II, ed. E. Bellorini, *Scrittori d'Italia*, vol. XXVII (Bari, 1912), pp. 11–12.

3.22 *Records, Broadcasts, etc.* Give a date if you can find it.

> D. Kern Holoman, jacket notes to Hector Berlioz, *Symphonie fantastique*, Chicago Symphony Orchestra/Claudio Abbado (Deutsche Grammophon Digital Stereo 410 895–1, 1984).

SHORT TITLES

3.23 After the complete citation has been given once, a frequently cited source may be abbreviated. We prefer this system to the use of the abbreviations *op. cit.* and *loc. cit.*

> [16]*Schumann–Brahms Briefe* I, 69.
> [17]Kalbeck, *Brahms* I, 198.
> [18]Litzmann, *Clara Schumann* II, 316–17.
> [19]"Historical Influences," pp. 6–7.

3.24 This is a particularly useful convention when dealing with the great definitive biographies.

> Raabe II, 70.   Boschot III, 285.   Budden I, 506.

REVIEW HEADS

3.25 The elements of information in a review head are separated by periods and include a page count.

> Theodor Adorno. *In Search of Wagner.* Translated by Rodney Livingstone. New York: Schocken Books, 1981. 159 pp.
>
> *Catalogue of the Mendelssohn Papers in the Bodleian Library, Oxford,* vol. 1: *Correspondence of Felix Mendelssohn Bartholdy and Others.* Compiled by Margaret Crum. (Musikbibliographische Arbeiten 7, gen. ed. Rudolf Elvers.) Tutzing: Hans Schneider, 1980. xiv, 374 pp.

ABBREVIATIONS

3.26 For the most part, *19th-Century Music* gives Latin abbreviations in roman type.

> Ibid.   i.e.   e.g.

3.27 *Ibid.* begins with a capital *I* only at the beginning of a sentence. In general, we much prefer the use of short titles for repeated citations. In any event, use *ibid.* only when footnotes are consecutive.

3.28 We try not to use *ff.* in a citation, since it implies that the author has not bothered to see where the relevant passage concludes. Where it is appropriately used, we give it in italics.

And indeed the Viennese paper found on fols. 125*ff.* is again of higher quality.

The new theme in mm. 59*ff.* begins with the same motive.

Holoman, *Autographs*, pp. 279*ff.*

3.29 Folios are identified by the abbreviation *fol.* and with the use of superscript characters for *recto* and *verso*.

MS 1163, fol. 52ᵛ, contains a listing of all the movements of the *Missa solemnis*.

3.30 For archival location, use the standard *RISM* abbreviation.

F-Pc D 17339 is a poignant dossier on the dissolution of the Société des Concerts.

PRINCIPLES OF ANNOTATION

3.31 Footnotes, which are expensive to paginate and difficult to control for accuracy, should be kept to a minimum. Adherence to the two rules of thumb that follow will drastically reduce the number of footnotes required.

3.32 Where possible, give page references in the running text (see 2.80–81).

True, the mention of Petrarch's name "gives us a reality instead of surrealism" (p. 121).

3.33 Where possible, conflate references into a single note at the end of a paragraph or section.

To limit our research to specialized music reviews would exclude many of our most precious reflections on the century's musical activities including, for example, those by Berlioz (who contributed regularly to the daily *Journal des Débats*—as did Castil-Blaze, Joseph d'Ortigue, Ernest Reyer, and Adolphe Jullien).[8]

(The note goes on collectively to summarize the tenure of each of these writers.)

3.34 Notes should, for the most part, be limited to the provision of references. Avoid the temptation to offer parenthetical or subsidiary discussions in the notes.

3.35 *Footnotes or Endnotes*. For works with copious musical examples, tables, or other such illustrative materials, authors must be prepared to have endnotes rather than foot-of-page notes; otherwise, the graceful design of individual page layouts becomes almost impossible. In general, current technology of publication favors endnotes over footnotes, especially for books and other long texts. It is a case where the economics of the situation simply takes precedence over philosophy. The advent of useful computerized paginating technology, however, may soon make the production of footnotes less expensive than it is at present.

3.36 By the same token, term papers and other shorter manuscripts probably look best with endnotes, and these are certainly less time-consuming than coping with the arrangement of footnotes on the typed page—unless, of course, your computer does it for you.

3.37 Manuscript for notes to be typeset should be *double-spaced* and be placed at the end of the article.

SAMPLE NOTES

3.38 The following are some randomly selected notes that demonstrate various aspects of our philosophy of citation:

[1]Abbiati, III, 26. Verdi wrote a curious letter to Léon Escudier on 30 June 1865 in which he raises the question of a Paris *Re Lear*. "Consider, if we were to chose *Re Lear*, we would have to be bound to Shakespeare and follow his footsteps rigorously. He is such a poet that one cannot touch him without robbing him of his powerful originality and character" (see J.-G. Prod'homme, "Lettres inédites de Léon Escudier," *Rivista musicale italiana* 35 [1928], 191).

[2]Mario Medici, Marcello Conati, and Marisa Casati, *Carteggio Verdi–Boito* (Parma, 1978), I, 150 (letter of 12 July 1889). Boito adds: "Their love ought to enliven everything and always in such a way that I would almost wish to drop the duet of the two lovers."

[3]For an analysis of the pervasive role of the descending third in the musical organization of the "Hammerklavier," see Charles Rosen, *The Classical Style* (New York, 1971), pp. 404–34. The importance of falling thirds in the Mass in general has been discussed by Joseph Schmidt-Görg in "Zur melodischen Einheit in

Beethoven's 'Missa solemnis'," in *Festschrift A. von Hoboken*, ed. Schmidt-Görg (Mainz, 1962), pp. 146*ff.*

[4]Recent research by Joshua Rifkin leads to the same result, that is, the establishment of four chronologically distinct compositional layers within the autograph (see Rifkin, "A Note on Schubert's Great C-Major Symphony," this journal 6 [1982], 13–16).

[5]Robert Schumann, "Neue Bahnen," *Neue Zeitschrift für Musik* 39 (1853), 185. This article has been translated many times; one of the most colorful (upon which I have drawn in my citations here) is "New Roads," in Robert Schumann, *On Music and Musicians*, ed. Konrad Wolff, trans. Paul Rosenfeld (New York, 1946), pp. 252–54.

[6]Isaiah Berlin, "The Concept of Scientific History," rpt. in *Concepts and Categories* (New York, 1979), pp. 103–42; see pp. 131–32.

4. Musical Examples

4.1 Musical examples should be deployed with great care to ensure accuracy in rendering the desired text. Most musical examples cut-and-pasted from xerox copies are useless; rather, they should be carefully edited, reduced, and recopied, then added to the manuscript on separate pages. The following conventions of style are intended largely for contributors to *19th-Century Music*, but careful study of them may be useful to student authors.

4.2 *19th-Century Music* is relatively generous with musical examples, particularly those limited in size to between one and four staves. Where possible, reduce musical examples to that dimension. These should be submitted on separate sheets, generally with one example per page, with careful attention to the *complete* legibility of photocopied material. Manuscript should be easily readable by the compositor at a distance of two feet. Manuscripts in ink are greatly preferable to those in pencil. The author's name should appear on each page, as musical examples are typeset separately. Text should be legibly written or typed, the correspondence between lyrics and notation clear, and syllable breaks made in accordance with the standard practice of the language. The accepted guidelines may be found in the current editions of *The Chicago Manual of Style, Hart's Rules for Compositors and Readers,* and *Webster's New Collegiate Dictionary.* Older music engravings often leave multisyllable words unbroken; our practice is to divide all syllables. Words may be broken by drawing vertical lines through the syllable breaks with colored pencil. Orthographic changes owing to word division must be taken into account: for example, the German Zucker becomes Zuk-ker. Any departure from modern spelling or standard word division should be noted in the margin of the manuscript.

It is best to keep the number, length, and complexity of musical examples to whatever minimum level still allows the readers to make their way through the author's reasoning. Musical examples are shockingly expensive and time-consuming, and errors slip past even the most perceptive in the process of publication.

4.3   The caption should be placed beneath the example; it should be as short as possible. Multiple-part examples are identified by lower-case letters at the upper left of the part. Measure numbers are generally included at the beginning of each line, or every five bars.

Example 1: *Les Préludes.*

Piano/Vocal Draft and Fair Copy

Published Version

Example 2

4.4   The following abbreviations, always in the singular, are used in our musical examples.

Fl.	Hn.	Timp.	Vn. I	S. or Sopr.
Ob.	Trpt.	S.D.	Vn. II	M.-S. or M.-Sopr.
E.h.	Trb.	B.D.	Vla.	C.-A. or Contr.
Cl.	Tuba	Cym.	Vc.	A. or Alto
Bsn.			Cb.	T. or Ten.
Ww.	Brass	Perc.	(or D.-B.)	B. or Bass
		Harp	Str.	
		Pf.		

Note that names of instruments are capitalized in the musical examples, though in the running text, where they would not be abbreviated, they would be given in lower-case.

4.5 Names of characters in a drama go in large and small capitals followed by a colon, placed above the staff.

Example 5

4.6 Reserve the standard lyre bracket for true piano parts and for such joined parts as violins and horns.

4.7 Otherwise, connect braces with standard straight brackets, or, preferably, none at all.

Example 3: *Faust* Symphony, first movement.

4.8 Rehearsal numbers and letters are given in boxes.

Example 10: *Der Rosenkavalier*, act 1, *Einleitung*.

4.9 Translations of texts, where appropriate, are given below the example, to the left, so as to avoid the problem of placing translated syllables beneath pitches.

For three days in Uglich cathedral I stood by the boy's body.

Example 12: *Boris Godunov*, p. 151.

4.10 For analytical graphs and related copy, the author should take care to specify the *exact* placement of characters on the staff. We welcome the submission of camera-ready copy of such materials.

4.11 In matters of notation, Gardner Read's *Music Notation: A Manual of Modern Practice* is our standard reference. Minor notational matters, such as stem and slur direction, need not be corrected on the manuscript; they will be set in accordance with modern practice by our engravers. If the contributor intends to have music set in nonstandard notation (e.g., a transcription of a composer's draft manuscript), he or she must communicate that intent on the manuscript.

4.12 The following are some interesting cases of musical examples published by *19th-Century Music*.

FURIES:	Du betäubst nicht unser Ohr.	(You do not deceive us. Open to me the dark
ORPHEUS:	Eröffnet mir das dunkle Thor.	portal. Never will this portal open. You,
FURIES:	Nimmer öffnet sich diess Thor.	strings, resonate in clear chorus.)
ORPHEUS:	Ihr Saiten rauscht im hellen Chor.	
	(lines 6–9)	

circle of thirds

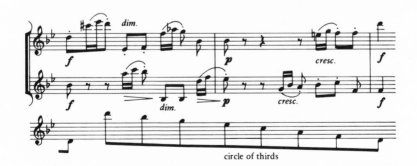

circle of thirds

Example 6

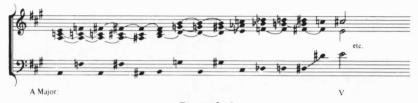

A Major: V

Example 1

Rigoletto: "La donna è mobile"

e _____ di _ pen - sier

Ex. 67: Bonci

e _____ di pen - sier

a. Schumann, Symphony in D Minor, I, m. 29.

b. Schumann, Symphony in D Minor, IV, m. 1.

c. Schumann, Violin Sonata in D Minor, I, mm. 44–45.

d. Schumann, *Faust* Overture, m. 16.

Example 6

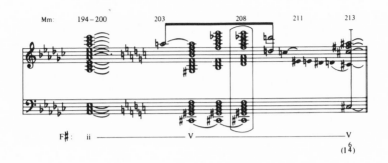

Mm: 194–200   203   208   211   213

F#:   ii ——————————————— V ————————————————— V
                                                           (14⁶)

---

a. "E' salvo!"

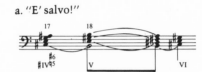

b. "Esultate!"

c. "Vittoria!"

d. "Venga la morte"

e. "Ah! la gioia m'innonda"

Example 2

Fugue Subject

Intervallic Basis of Fugue Subject   "Credo" Motive

Figure 1

5. Tables and Illustrations

5.1 Tables should be submitted on separate sheets of paper, with the author's name appearing on each sheet. These are typeset separately. The conditions noted in the second paragraph of 4.2 above apply just as well to tables as to musical examples. If they can be avoided, they should be: complex tables, in particular, are nightmares for author, editor, and typesetter.

5.2 Tables wider than about 100 characters will not fit our pages; seven columns or more stretches the capabilities of the typesetting system.

5.3 The following are some examples of tables which have appeared in *19th-Century Music*.

Table 1
PERRIN'S OPÉRA-COMIQUE REGISTERS AND VOLUMES
FROM OTHER ENTERPRISES

Enterprise	Brief Description	Vol. Nos.	Period
Opéra-Comique	Daily accounts	295–97	Feb. 1846–Apr. 1848
	Payments to authors	299B–C	May 1848–May 1850
	Other accounts	299A, 299D–J	May 1848–Nov. 1857
Théâtre Feydeau	Payments to authors	179	June 1800–Mar. 1801
Théâtre-Italien	Accounts	288–93	1830/31–1838/39
	Index to suppliers' bills	282	May 1835–Jan. 1842
	Accounts	281	Dec. 1843–Oct. 1845
	List of subscribers	283	1846/47
	Accounts	285–86	Oct. 1853–July 1855
Théâtre Lyrique, boulevard du Temple	Accounts	300–04	Sept. 1853–June 1856

Table 2

DATA ON THE RECORDINGS

Ex. #	Artist	Aria	Original*	Place/date recorded	LP transfer
1	Stracciari	"Dio di giuda"	Col D12470	Milan, 1925	99–29
2	De Lucia	"Come rugiada"	Phono M 1811	Naples, 1917	GV 575
3	Caffetto		Berliner 52462	Milan, 1900	
4	Scampini		GC 2-52611	Milan, 1908	
5	Sembrich	"Ernani involami"	Col 1364	New York, 1903	Y2 35232
6	Caligaris		G&T 53326	Milan, 1904	
7	Talexis		Fono 92111	Milan, 1908	
8	Gabbi		Col 10124	Milan, 1903	
9	Battistini/ Corsi	"Da quel di"	G&T 054103	Milan, 1907	CO 326, GV 100

5.4 For all other illustrative material, original copy of the highest quality should be provided by the author. For virtually all illustrative matter other than photographs of individuals, we much prefer receiving photo-mechanical transfers (PMTs) to glossy photographs. Captions should be typed on a separate page.

5.5 It is the author's responsibility to secure permission to reprint copyrighted material. A copy of the letter authorizing such reprinting should be sent to the editorial office.

5.6 The following are some examples of illustrative matter which has appeared in *19th-Century Music:*

Plate 1: Richard Strauss and Cäcilie Wenzel in 1886.

4ʙ
fol. 9ᵛ

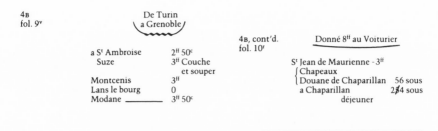

De Turin
a Grenoble

a Sᵗ Ambroise	2ᶠᶠ 50ᶜ
Suze	3ᶠᶠ Couche
	et souper
Montcenis	3ᶠᶠ
Lans le bourg	0
Modane ———	3ᶠᶠ 50ᶜ

4ʙ, cont'd.
fol. 10ʳ

Donné 8ᶠᶠ au Voiturier

Sᵗ Jean de Maurienne - 3ᶠᶠ
{ Chapeaux
{ Douane de Chaparillan 56 sous
  a Chaparillan 2ƒ4 sous
  déjeuner

4c
fol. 10ᵛ

Edvard Munch: *The Shriek* (1896). Lithograph, printed in black. Sheet
20⅝″ × 16¹³⁄₁₆″

Collection, The Museum of Modern Art, New York. Matthew T. Mellon Fund
Reproduced by permission

Folio*	Content
1	*Liebesbotschaft*, 1ʳ–1ᵛ.
2	*Kriegers Ahnung*, 2ᵛ–4ʳ.
3	
4	*Frühlingssehnsucht*, 4ᵛ–5ᵛ, st. 9.
5	*Ständchen*, 5ᵛ, st. 11–6ᵛ, st. 9.
6	*Aufenthalt*, 6ᵛ, st. 11–8ʳ.
7	
8	*In der Ferne*, 8ᵛ–9ᵛ, st. 9.
9	*Abschied*, 9ᵛ, st. 12–12ᵛ.
10	
11	
12	
13	*Der Atlas*, 13ʳ–13ᵛ.
14	*Ihr Bild*, 14ʳ.
	Das Fischermädchen, 14ᵛ–15ʳ.
15	*Die Stadt*, 15ᵛ–16ʳ, st. 6.
16	*Am Meer*, 16ʳ, st. 9–17ʳ, st. 3.
17	*Der Doppelgänger*, 17ʳ, st. 6–17ᵛ.
18	*Die Taubenpost*, 18ʳ–20ʳ.
19	
20	
	[20ᵛ–21ᵛ blank]
21	

* Fols. 1–19 are of paper-type [Winter] VIId, fols. 20–21 of VIIIa; see Winter, "Paper Studies," pp. 253– 55.

Table 1: Fascicle Structure of *Schwanengesang* Autograph.

All illustrations reproduced by permission of owner.

1. Sketch from Cello part to the *Mélologue*, H. 55A.
F-Pc ms 17465.

6. The Printed Program

CONCERTS

6.1 The heading of the concert program should list the presenter, the performing group, and the solo artists.

University of California, Davis
The Department of Music presents the

UCD Early Music Ensemble
David Nutter, director
with
Jeffrey Thomas, tenor

Include the names of financial underwriters, if appropriate.

6.2 The foot of the program should give the time, date, and venue of the performance. Make certain to include the year, as this information is required by the tax authorities; without the inclusion of the year, moreover, the concert program is virtually worthless as a historical document.

Sunday, 26 October 1986   Church of St. Martin, Episcopal
8:00 P.M.   Hawthorn Lane, Davis

6.3 The standard listing of a work in a concert program gives a formal title with key and index identifier, the composer's full name, and the composer's dates. Movements follow, with foreign words italicized.

Orchestral Suite No. 3 in D Major,   Johann Sebastian Bach
   BWV 1068   (1685–1750)

Ouverture
Air
Gavotte I
Gavotte II
Bourrée
Gigue

Rhapsody on a Theme of Paganini,   Sergei Rachmaninov
   opus 43, for Piano and Orchestra   (1873–1943)

Four Dance-Episodes from *Rodeo*   Aaron Copland
                                           (b. 1900)

   Buckaroo Holiday
   Corral Nocturne
   Saturday Night Waltz
   Hoe Down

6.4 For a movement identified by both a title and a tempo indication, use a colon after the title.

Symphony No. 3 in E♭ Major   Ludwig van Beethoven
   ("Eroica"), opus 55   (1770–1827)

   Allegro con brio
   Marcia funebre: Adagio assai
   Scherzo: Allegro vivace
   Finale: Allegro molto

6.5 For a movement embracing a major change of tempo, as in a movement with a slow introduction and a succeeding Allegro, separate the two with a semicolon.

Concerto for Piano and Orchestra   Piotr Tchaikovsky
   No. 1 in B♭ Minor, opus 23   (1840–93)

   Allegro non troppo e molto maestoso; Allegro con spirito
   Andante simplice
   Allegro con fuoco

6.6 It is, however, cumbersome to list a multitude of tempo changes. For the finale to Beethoven's Ninth, for example, it should suffice to list the tempi through the beginning of the exposition, though even this solution is not especially pretty.

Symphony No. 9 in D Minor,   Ludwig van Beethoven
   opus 125, with a closing chorus   (1770–1827)
   on Schiller's "Ode to Joy"

   Allegro non troppo, un poco maestoso
   Molto vivace
   Adagio molto e cantabile
   Presto; Allegro assai; Presto; Recitativo; Allegro assai vivace;
     Andante maestoso; Allegro energico; Allegro ma non troppo

6.7 It is appropriate to translate movement titles that might not otherwise be understood, particularly if they are not translated elsewhere in the program.

Concerto for Orchestra   Béla Bartók
                                                    (1881–1945)

    Introduzione
    Giuoco delle coppie ("Game of Pairs")
    Elegia
    Intermezzo interrotto ("Interrupted Intermezzo")
    Finale

6.8 For first performances, it is customary to give the date of composition and indicate the festivity of the occasion.

    The Big Bang and Beyond (1985)   Steven Mackey
    (First Performance)   (b. 1953)

6.9 For works that tell a story, it is helpful to list the incidents in the program.

    The Moldau (*Vltava*)   Bedřich Smetana
    from *My Fatherland* (*Ma Vlast*)   (1824–84)

    The Two Sources of the Moldau—Forest Hunt—Peasant Wedding—Moonlight: Nymphs' Dance—St. John's Rapids—The Moldau in Its Greatest Breadth—Vyšehrad

6.10 Performances arranged by special permission should be so noted in the program.

Symphony No. 2 in D Minor, opus 42   George Onslow
                                                   (1784–1853)

    Allegro vivace ed energico
    Andante grazioso, con moto
    Menuetto: Allegro
    Finale: Presto agitato

By kind arrangement with the Edwin A. Fleisher Collection, Free Library of Philadelphia.

6.11 The following is a complete program page for a concert of the Sacramento Symphony Orchestra. Note their use of a style that favors flush-left alignment and uses composers' last names only.

The Sacramento Symphony Orchestra
Carter Nice, Music Director
1984–85 Season

This concert has been made possible in part by a generous gift
from the A. K. Tsakopoulous Fund and Friends of the Sacra-
mento Hellenic Community.

Saturday, September 22, 8:30 p.m.
Sacramento Community Center Theater

CARTER NICE, Conductor
PANAYIS LYRAS, Piano

GLINKA
Overture to *Russlan and Ludmilla*

SCHUMANN
Concerto for Piano and Orchestra in A Minor, opus 54
  Allegro affettuoso
  Intermezzo: Andantino grazioso
  Allegro vivace
  Mr. Lyras, piano

Intermission

BRAHMS
Symphony No. 2 in D Major, opus 73
  Allegro non troppo
  Adagio non troppo
  Allegretto grazioso quasi andantino
  Allegro con spirito

OPERAS

6.12 Opera billings should include the name of the librettist.

Vincenzo Bellini

I Capuleti e i Montecchi

Lyric Tragedy in Two Acts
Libretto by Felice Romani

TEXTS AND TRANSLATIONS

6.13 Texts and translations are mandatory for texted works. The
lights in the house should be set to a level that will allow follow-

ing the text. Due credit should be given the translator, and appropriate permissions secured. Texts are most usefully presented with the original language and the English translation in facing columns. Have the typist or typesetter take care to put page-turns where they will not distract from the performance.

Aux prodiges de la Victoire	To honor the prodigious victors
Qu'un autre consacre ses chants,	May another poet devote his songs:
Que ses vers mâles et touchans	Virile, moving verses
Célèbrent les fils de la gloire.	To celebrate the sons of Glory.
En vain leur courage indompté	In vain their invincible courage
Nous gagnait cent et cent batailles;	Won us countless battles
Le crime au sein de nos murailles	While the traitor in our own walls
Allait tuer la Liberté!	Was about to destroy Liberty.
Refrain:	*Refrain:*
Chantons la Liberté, couronnons sa statue	Sing we to Liberty, crown we her statue.
Comme un nouveau Titan le crime est foudroyé:	Like a new titan, the traitor has been struck down.
Relève, relève ta tête abattue,	Raise, o France, thy bowed head,
O France, à tes destins Dieu lui-même a veillé.	For God himself has watched over thy destiny.

—trans. DKH

6.14 For long texted works, where members of the audience would otherwise be flipping back and forth in the program, it is sometimes graceful to place program order, text, and note together.

[Handel: *Israel in Egypt*]

Part the First
The Exodus

1–2
Recitative and Chorus

Now there arose a new king over Egypt, which knew not Joseph. And he set over Israel taskmasters to afflict them with burthens. And they made them serve with rigour. (*Exodus* 1:8, 11, 13.)

And the children of Israel sighed by reason of the bondage. And their cry came up unto God. They oppressed them with burthens, and made them serve with rigour. (*Exodus* 2:23.)

After the tenor's short recitative, a poignant chorus of Israel's burdens. Cast in the dark key of C minor, it opens with a brief solo statement by the alto, followed by the uplifting theme for "And their cry came up unto God" and another theme, treated fugally, for "they oppress'd them with burthens." The long, haunting chorus returns again and again to the word "sighed," palpitating with the agony of the situation. At the end we hear a simultaneous statement in all eight voices of the lament rising heavenward.

[Bach: B-Minor Mass]

Part II

Symbolum Nicenum (Nicene Creed)

1

Credo in unum Deum.   I believe in one God.

Five-part chorus, violins I–II, continuo.

"A dazzling array," says Rifkin, "of imitative configurations" for the chorus and violins, supported by the faster-moving bass part and based on a Gregorian plainsong intonation in use at the time. Bach may have first written the music as an introduction to the work of another composer.

ROSTERS OF PERSONNEL

6.15 Personnel rosters follow the rules of common sense. Musicians tend to be grateful to have their names listed as they themselves prefer, though in one case we denied a fellow named Boom-Boom his sobriquet.

THE CHAMBER SINGERS

Soprano	Alto	Tenor
Kristi Brown	Naomi Braun	Carlo Delumpa
Judith Cho	Donna Di Grazia	Terry Fleury
Patricia Hallam	Jeanne Hirota	**Bass**
Lisa Lambro	Mary Ann Long	David Dyer
		Timothy Hanson
		Lee Riggs

THE ORCHESTRA

Violin I
Cynthia Bates,
  concertmaster
Ken Hayashi
Susan Coyle
Ken Murai
Judy Riggs

Violin II
Henry Hsu,
  principal
Amy Merchant
Alanna Battat
Joan Cook
Gabrielle O'Byrne

Viola
Debbie Thurmond,
  principal
Karen Yee
Kathrine Gardner

Cello
Alice Swan,
  solo continuo
Elizabeth Tucker
Janet Ishida

Bass
Anton Uhle

Oboe
Caryn Hough
Lori Ann Joe

Bassoon
Rebecca J. Littman

Trumpet
Curt Buttke
Arjay Raffety

Timpani
Darin Wilson

Carrie K. Brothers, *continuo*

PROGRAM NOTES

6.16 Program notes should briefly recount the circumstances of composition and first performance of the work, its scoring, and, if useful, brief information on its publication. Rusty anecdotes and preciousness should be avoided, as should difficult analytical terminology. Musical examples in program notes are uncommon. Try to suggest to the audience two or three particular things to listen for, in an attempt to engage their ears.

Quite brief program notes can be effective in the following notice on Berlioz's arrangement of Rouget de Lisle's *La Marseillaise.*

> Berlioz prepared the first of his two settings of Rouget de Lisle's *Marseillaise* in the aftermath of the July 1830 Revolution. It was published by the Paris firm of Maurice Schlesinger in late 1830. The work is scored for pairs of clarinets and bassoons, four horns, six trumpets, three trombones and tuba, six timpani, bass drum, strings, and chorus. We perform the first of six stanzas.

Or this, concerning Berlioz's *Marche funèbre pour la dernière scène d'Hamlet:*

> This little-known but spectacular work of Berlioz's was prepared in conjunction with a French translation of *Hamlet* scheduled for presentation in 1844 at the Odéon Theater, the very edifice where he had first seen Harriet Smithson play the role of Ophelia in 1827. (He composed two other works for the new production:

the moving song of Ophelia's drowning as offered by Queen Gertrude at the end of act IV, called *La Mort d'Ophélie*; and music for the dumb-show, which has not been preserved.) The funeral march, which Berlioz never heard performed, was to be played after the last line of text, as the four captains bear Hamlet's body from the stage. It is scored for full orchestra, muffled drums, chorus singing the syllable *"ah,"* and, at the climax, a volley of rifle fire, as directed by Shakespeare. (We did not bring the Army ROTC, Davis detachment, to Vancouver, though they participated in a previous performance.)

The finished autograph carries the date of 22 September 1848, just three weeks after the death of the composer's father. Presumably the work can be thought of as a tribute to the grand old man who had contributed so much to his son's poetic instincts.

6.17 Michael Steinberg, in the course of his work with the Boston and San Francisco Symphony Orchestras, has developed a style of program annotation in which the basic facts of the work are presented in italic type in the first paragraph, always in the same general order. Audiences have learned to turn first to these paragraphs and generally have them under their belt by the time the concert starts. The following extract concerns Stravinsky's *Reynard*.

> *Igor Fedorovich Stravinsky was born at Oranienbaum, Russia, now Lomonosov in the Leningrad Region, on 5 June/old style or 17 June/new style 1882 and died in New York City on 6 April 1971. He began the score of* Reynard *at Château d'Oex, Switzerland, in the spring of 1915 and completed it, according to his notation on the final page of the manuscript vocal score, at "Morges, 1 August 1916, at noon, sky without clouds." The work was first given at the Paris Opera by Serge Diaghilev's Russian Ballet on 18 May 1922: Ernest Ansermet conducted, the choreography was by Bronislava Nijinska (who also danced the title role), and the production was by Michel Larionov. The work came to the United States the following year, when a concert performance was given in New York on 2 December 1923 in the French translation of C. F. Ramuz. The present performances are the first by the San Francisco Symphony. The score calls for two tenors and two basses, flute (doubling piccolo), oboe (doubling English horn), clarinet (doubling E-flat clarinet), bassoon, two horns, trumpet, cimbalom, timpani, cymbals, bass drum, snare drum, tambourine with and without jingles, triangle and a quintet of solo strings (two violins, viola, cello, bass). The cimbalom is a gypsy dulcimer. It is replaced in these performances by a doctored piano, an expedient for which a number of Stravinsky's own performances provide a precedent. Paul Connelly is the pianist.*
>
> If someone in your family bought a Singer sewing machine early this century, she (or he) helped pay for *Reynard*. . . .

7. Preparing Copy to Submit Electronically

7.1 *19th-Century Music* welcomes and indeed strongly encourages transmission of manuscript by electronic means. We submit virtually all manuscript to our typesetter on computer disks. Three major steps in the editorial process are simplified when we receive the copy on computer disks prepared by the author, thus vastly improving the quality of the galley proofs authors must correct.

7.2 The *19th-Century Music* office presently uses IBM-type computers and the MS-DOS operating system. We are prepared to convert floppy disks prepared with almost any program based on CP/M, Apple, UNIX, or MS-DOS operating systems.

7.3 *First submissions should be in the form of traditional manuscript.* After an article has been accepted for publication *and* after the final text has been agreed to by both editor and author, it is useful for the editorial office to receive a floppy disk containing text prepared according to the following rules.

7.4 *Submit generic copy with all printer commands removed.* The critical rule is to omit commands specific to individual word-processing programs. Submit a file saved in the most generic manner your program allows. Specifically:

> Omit page numbers; pagination off
> Justification off
> Hyphenation off
> Single-spaced
> Single spaces after ends of sentences
> No margin or tab set
> No overstrikes
> No superscripts or subscripts
> No underlining
> No block indentations
> Distinguish between l and 1, and 0 and O.
> Type the ellipsis mark with spaces: . . . , not ... .

7.5 *Commands recognized by the typesetter.* Our computing systems recognize all ASCII-II characters, hard carriage returns,
tabs, and the following commands. Note that these commands,
inasmuch as they are embedded in the running text, are convert-
ible under any typesetting system; they are simple to use, easy
to remember, and widely recognized.

@	=	Begin italic
+ + +	=	Begin boldface
@@	=	Begin bold italic
+ +	=	Begin small caps (type lower-case letters)
+	=	End italic, boldface, bold italic, small caps
=A	=	flat: ♭
=B	=	box for rehearsal numbers or letters: 295=B = 295
=b	=	black box for holding space: ∎
=C	=	center
=F	=	$\frac{6}{4}$
=L	=	flush left
=N	=	natural: ♮
=n	=	sharp: ♯
=p	=	pound sign: £
=R	=	flush right
=S	=	section mark: §
=s	=	asterisk: *
=X	=	anything you cannot find in the codes
=(	=	open square bracket [
=)	=	close square bracket]
=–	=	*en*-dash: –
––	=	*em*-dash: —
=&	=	+
!A	=	acute accent: e!A = é
!C	=	cedilla: c!C = ç
!G	=	grave accent: a!G = à
!i	=	no-dot i: ma!i!Xtre = maître
!L	=	Polish character: Ł
!l	=	Polish character: ł
!M	=	macron: a!M = ā
!S	=	German character: ß
!T	=	tilde: n!T = ñ
!U	=	umlaut: u!U = ü
!V	=	hacek: s!V = š
!X	=	circumflex: e!X = ê

A!E	=	Æ	O!E	=	Œ
a!e	=	æ	o!e	=	œ
A!O	=	Å	O!/	=	Ø
A!o	=	å	o!/	=	ø

(SPACE)	=	line-space
[SUP/#]	=	superscript: cited in @Grove. + [SUP/27] = cited in *Grove*.[27]
[SUB/#]	=	subscript

7.6   *Format Codes.* The following format codes are specific to *19th-Century Music*. The production staff is grateful when they are entered by the author (*after* the final text is agreed upon).

[F1]   Title Heads (24 points)
[F2]   Author Heads (12 points) caps, flush left
[F3]   Begin text (10 points, leaded 12)
[F4]   Begin block citation (9 points, leaded 10), non-indented, filled
[F5]   Small cap subtitle, centered, preceded by single line-space
[F6]   Begin poetry extract, indented: 9/10 block, unfilled
[F7]   Line-space plus return to 10/12 text, no new paragraph
[F8]   Line-space plus return to 10/12 text, new paragraph
[F9]   Footnotes (8 points, leaded 9)
[F10] Review head (24 points)
[F11] Review title (20 points)
[F12] Review author (11 points)
[F13] Citation of books reviewed (9 points, leaded 11)
[F14] Begin 10/12 text with indent but no line-space
[F15] Copyright paragraph (inserted by editors)
[F16] Same as [F4] but with a measure of 30 picas, used for citations from libretti, with a tab separating the character name from the spoken text

7.7   End the file with footnotes, captions, and the like.

7.8   Tables and other material unsuited to electronic transmission should be submitted as hard copy.

7.9   *Guard against disaster.* Submit one copy of the floppy disk, keeping another copy; specify operating system and word-processing program used.

7.10 The following example shows a sample typeset passage followed by a visual rendering of the electronic copy from which it was prepared:

CLIFFORD CRANNA

Rossini. *Quelques Riens pour album.* Edited by Marvin Tartak. Edizione Critica delle Opere di Gioachino Rossini VII/7. Pesaro: Fondazione Rossini, 1982.xxi., 223 pp.

The set of twenty-four witty and delightful piano pieces to which Rossini gave the self-deprecating title "Trivia for an Album" are among some 150 small-scale works (piano solos, songs, small ensembles) called by their composer his

Péchés de vieillesse ("sins of old age"). These pieces were the products of a final surge of creative activity in Rossini's last decade (1858–68), during which the composer, having regained his health after years of illness, often presided as the host of musical *soirées* given in his Paris home and at his villa in Passy. The *Péchés* were not for publication but rather intended as private entertainment for his guests. Among them

[F12]CLIFFORD CRANNA=L

[F13]Rossini. aQuelques Riens pour album.+ Edited by Marvin Tartak. Edizione Critica delle Opere di Gioacchino Rossini VII/7. Pesaro: Fondazione Rossini, 1982. xxi, 223 pp.

[F14]The set of twenty-four witty and delightful piano pieces to which Rossini gave the self-deprecating title "Trivia for an Album+ are among some 150 small-scale works (piano solos, songs, small ensembles) called by their composer his aPe!Ache!As de viellesse+ ("sins of old age"). These pieces were the products of a final surge of creative activity in Rossini's last decade (1858=-68), during which the composer, having regained his health after years of illness, often presided as the host of musical asoire!Aes+ given in his Paris home and at his villa in Passy. The aPe!Ache!As+ were not for publication but rather indended as private entertainment for his guests. Among them

APPENDIX: PROBLEM WORDS

a cappella (italic; note spelling)
acknowledgement
ad hominem (roman)
aegis
Aeschylus
aesthetic
afterthought
afterward (no *s*)
alter ego (two words)
appoggiatura
a priori (roman)
à propos (roman, two words, with accent)
archaeologist
avant-garde (hyphen, roman)

bar line (two words)
bas-relief (hyphen, roman)
Beaumarchais's
benefited
Berlioz's
bizarrerie (roman)
bona fide (roman)
Brahms's
bulrushes

caesura (no ligature)
canceled, canceling, cancellation
Christlike
concerti, concertos (per author)
consensus
contrapuntist (not contrapuntalist)
correspondence
cortège

D.C. (periods, no space)
debatable
debut (no accent)
de-emphasis
deity
dénouement (with accent, roman)
discreet (careful)
discrete (separate)
dramatis personae (italic)
dreamlike
Dussek

elegiac
elite (no accent)
end-product
en route (roman)
étude (accent, roman)

focuses, focusing, focused (one *s*)
fulfill, fulfillment

grace note (two words)
granddaughter (one word, no hyphen)
gratis (italic)

herculean (lower-case)
high point (two words)

imaginable
indexes (not indices)
interchangeability
interrelated (no hyphen)

judgement

Krakow (not Cracow)

59

Leitmotiv, (pl.) Leitmotive or
    leitmotivs
littérateur (italic, accent)
Livorno (not Leghorn)

maneuver
Missa solemnis (italic, 2nd word
    lower-case)
modeled
motive or motif, (pl.) motives,
    (adj.) motivic
motto, (pl.) mottoes

naive (no accent)
naiveté (one accent, roman)
Neoplatonic
Neapolitan
nonconforming (one word)
noteheads (one word)

obbligato (roman, two *b*s)
oneself
onomatopoetic
opéra-comique (roman),
    (pl.) opéras-comiques
opera-goer
opera seria (italic), (pl.) *opere
    serie*
ophicleide (no accent)

palette
pejorative
penciled
pitch class (no hyphen)
Prač (not Pratsch)
précis (with accent)
preconscious (no hyphen)
preeminent (no hyphen)
premiere (no accent)
premises
prima donna (roman)
profited, profiting
program (never programme)
protégé (two accents)

rearrange
recreate
re-emphasize (hyphen)
re-establish (hyphen)
reintroduce
relevant
repertoire (not repertory)
résumé (two accents)
rivaled
role (no accent)

Shakespearean (not Shakespear-
    ian)
side step (noun)
sidestep (verb)
sizable
skepticism
skillful
soft-pedaled
soulless (no hyphen)
staff, (pl.) staves
status quo (roman)
straightforward (no hyphen)
straw man (two words)
subject matter
subtitle (no hyphen)
supersede

Tchaikovsky
theater
thoroughbass (one word)
thoroughgoing (one word)
tour de force (italic)
toward (no *s*)
traveled, traveling

underrate (no hyphen)
unmistakable
upturn (one word)

vainglorious
vice versa (roman, no hyphen)
Virgil

vis-à-vis (roman, accent, hy-
    phens)
voice leading (no hyphen),
    but "parallel voice-leading"
von Bülow

Washington, D.C. (no space)
whereabouts
willful